Surviving in the Frozen Forest

Written by Kerrie Shanahan

Flying Start
to Literacy®

T0363474

Contents

Introduction

Some forests are covered in snow and ice for most of the year. These forests are near the North Pole. They are called taiga forests.

For a short time during summer, the snow and ice melt, but the forest is still very, very cold.

Not many animals can survive in a taiga forest, because it is so cold and there is not much food.

But moose can survive. They can live in the taiga forest all year round, because they can stay warm, find food and stay safe.

Chapter 1:
Living in the forest

Keeping warm

In winter, when it is very cold, moose can stay warm.

Moose have two layers of fur. The bottom layer of fur is woolly and short. The top layer is long and thick. In winter, their fur grows even longer and thicker.

Moving around

In winter, the snow in the taiga forest is very thick. It can be hard for animals to walk in thick snow, because they sink into it.

But moose can walk in thick snow. They have two wide, flat toes on each foot. This helps them to walk through the snow and not sink in too deep.

two wide, flat toes

Chapter 2: Finding food

Moose only eat plants. Because they are such big animals, they have to eat lots of plants.

Summer foods

In summer, when the snow and ice melt, lots of plants grow. There is plenty of food for the moose to eat. They eat leaves and berries.

Moose eat a lot of food in summer, and they store this food as fat. They survive on their fat when there is very little food in winter.

In summer, moose also eat the plants
that grow in lakes and rivers.

Moose are good swimmers
and can dive under the water.
They can swim to the bottom of the lake
and eat the plants that grow there.

Moose can stay under the water for up to 30 seconds.

13

Winter foods

In winter in the taiga forest, everything is covered in snow and ice. There is not much food.

Moose eat any plants they can find. They eat the bark and twigs of these plants.

Moose spend much of their day scrounging for food.

Moose also eat moss. In winter, moss is under the snow. Moose dig into the snow. Then they can graze on the moss.

Chapter 3: Staying safe

Moose are very big animals. There are not many animals that can attack and kill a moose. So moose do not have many predators.

Animals that do hunt moose will attack a young moose or an old, sick moose.

Packs of wolves will hunt together to attack a moose.

Hearing

Moose keep their young safe from predators by using their senses. They have good hearing and they can move their ears around. This helps them to know if a predator is nearby.

Smell

Moose also have a good sense of smell. They can smell a predator from a long way off.

Even when moose are sleeping, they can smell predators nearby. When this happens, they wake up.

Run away or stay and fight?

When a predator attacks a moose, the moose will either run away or stay and fight. Moose are fast runners and some moose will run away when attacked. But most moose stay and fight.

A moose fights the predator by kicking it. Male moose have antlers. They run at the predator and use their antlers to attack it.

Conclusion

The taiga forest is covered in snow and ice for most of the year. This makes it a hard place for most animals to live.

But moose are able to find food in the forest and stay safe from predators. And they can stay warm.

They can survive in the taiga forest.

Glossary

antlers   Male moose grow two large horns on their heads, which are called antlers.

graze   To graze is to eat small amounts of food all day.

predators   Predators are animals that hunt and kill other animals for food.

senses   The senses are hearing, seeing, smelling, taste and touch. The senses give animals information.

survive   To survive is to be able to keep living, even when it is very difficult.